T0208643

Living Life's Journey through what is Written

The Book of Sermons

Apostle Ebony L. Underwood

authorHOUSE

AuthorHouse™
1663 Liberty Drive
Bloomington, IN 47403
www.authorhouse.com
Phone: 833-262-8899

© 2022 Apostle Ebony L. Underwood. All rights reserved.

No part of this book may be reproduced, stored in a retrieval system, or transmitted by any means without the written permission of the author.

Published by AuthorHouse 04/20/2022

ISBN: 978-1-6655-5781-8 (sc)
ISBN: 978-1-6655-5779-5 (hc)
ISBN: 978-1-6655-5780-1 (e)

Print information available on the last page.

Any people depicted in stock imagery provided by Getty Images are models, and such images are being used for illustrative purposes only.
Certain stock imagery © Getty Images.

This book is printed on acid-free paper.

Because of the dynamic nature of the Internet, any web addresses or links contained in this book may have changed since publication and may no longer be valid. The views expressed in this work are solely those of the author and do not necessarily reflect the views of the publisher, and the publisher hereby disclaims any responsibility for them.

Scripture taken from the New King James Version®. Copyright © 1982 by Thomas Nelson. Used by permission. All rights reserved.

CONTENTS

INTRODUCTION

Dear People of God,

Often times we can see things happen in life and often wonder, how will I get through? Can I at all make it? Reading this book will help you to understand, even through the challenges of life and troubles we may face, our eternal and faithful God will always have His Word available to us. The bible declares, the earth will pass away but the Word of God will stand forever. As you read this book, open your mind to see there is no trial nor tribulation that will overtake them that believe in Jesus Christ. It's important as born- again believers that we live our life Journey through what is written. Let us hold fast to the confession of our faith. I pray you enjoy this Journey with mc.

DEDICATION

I dedicate this book to my Lord and Savior Jesus Christ. He is the reason why all of this is possible. Also, to all born- again believers. Those that are striving to live according to what is written in the scriptures. I would also like to give special thanks to my best friend and amazing husband, Pastor Mark Underwood. To my loving daughter, Minister Lashonda Jackson and my two beautiful Granddaughters, Desiree and Laila. To my church family (The Hub) who loves me and supports my vision.

CHAPTER 1

Completely Changed by the Power of the Gospel

The power of the gospel is the only way a lifestyle leading to destruction can really change. I believe through and by my own testimony, the only way true transformation can take place is by your submission to the written word of God. I was headed down a dangerous path that was not recognized as dangerous, but it was leading to hell. The only way you can be rescued is receiving salvation. We must understand Jesus came in the flesh to give us eternal life, freedom from sins control and a permanent home with Him and Glory. In the gospel of John chapter 1 the first verse says, in the beginning was the Word and the Word was with God and the Word was God. Jesus is the logos. Logos in its definition by way of the Bible in the Greek is transcribed as reason, word, speech, or principal. In Greek philosophy, it related to universal, divine reason or the mind of God. The gospel of John connected this Greek term with the nature in existence of God and Jesus Christ (Christianity.com Editorial Staff).

Jesus embodied that total message (the gospel) the Good News of Jesus Christ. That is why He is called the logos or the word of God. Hebrews 4:12 NKJV it says For the word of God is living and powerful, and sharper than any two-edged sword, piercing even to the division of soul and spirit, and a joints and marrow, and is a discerner of the thoughts and intents of the heart. Jesus showed the link between the written Word of God and Himself, in that He is the subject of the written word because He is the Word. The Bible declares the Word of God is living and powerful, we know Jesus, He is alive and He is living. The Bible speaks of him being powerful. In Revelation 19:6 NKJV And I heard, as it were, the voice of a great multitude, as the sound of many waters and as the sound of mighty thunderings, saying, "Alleluia! For the Lord God Omnipotent reigns! The word omnipotent comes from to Latin words, omnis, meaning all, and poetnia or potens which means power. I've said all of that to say, the only way my life, your life and anyone's life is going to transform will be only by the Power of the Gospel, the Good News of Jesus Christ.

Apostle Paul was one of the examples in the bible of being completely changed by the Power of the Gospel. Before becoming an Apostle, this man's life was going in the wrong direction. Apostle Paul whose name was Saul at that time was on his way on the road to Damascus to persecute the church and take them captive. He had no clue this dangerous road he was traveling will soon come to an end. When you are controlled by sin, you do not realize the state or condition you are in because sin blinds you. One day on a mission that Paul thought was right was the day Jesus was going to meet him. According to Acts 9 verses 3 & 4NKJV says, As he journeyed he came near Damascus, and suddenly a light shone around him from heaven 4th verse says, Then he fell to the ground, and heard a voice saying to him, "Saul Saul, why are you persecuting Me?" That day was the day Saul met Jesus. Remember Jesus is the Word, He is the logos. When you come in to contact with the written word you will be changed, when you accept it. Apostle Paul was changed on that day. His encounter with Jesus changed his life completely.

Change means in KJV dictionary to cause to turn or pass from one state to another; to alter or make different; to change the heart or life, to shift. There was a shift on the road of Damascus. He was on his way to do what he thought was right, but when he met Jesus, his whole plan was altered. His heart was changed. Suddenly he didn't want to hurt those that was serving Christ. He was to join forces with them and follow Christ. Just as Jesus did it for Paul, myself and many others He will do it for you.

CHAPTER 2

Your Faith Grows in Unfamiliar Places

As a born-again believer of Jesus Christ, we are to grow and flourish. Many times, we experience some challenges in our walk with Jesus. The bible says in 2 Peter 3:18 NKJV but grow in the grace and knowledge of our Lord and Savior Jesus Christ. To Him be all the glory both now and forever. Amen. The Bible is letting us know, those who are born again are expected to grow. The Lord begin to show me that your faith grows in unfamiliar places. We must keep in mind that we are on a journey. Also We will be in some unfamiliar places that challenges our faith to grow. The word unfamiliar in the Webster dictionary means not having any knowledge of something. Even in not having the knowledge of something there still should be a trust in Jesus. Just because it's unfamiliar to us does not mean it's unfamiliar to Him. In the book of Isaiah 46:9-10 NKJV it says, Remember the former things of old, For I am God, and there is no other; I am God, and there is none like Me, Declaring the end from the beginning, And from ancient times things that are not yet done, Saying, 'My counsel shall stand, And I will do all My pleasure,'

The Lord God knows all things. He is Omniscient. The Bible verse declared our end from the beginning is known by him. We just have to grow in faith and continue to believe that if it is written, if Jesus spoke it, and He is faithful, and true then we can continue even in an unfamiliar place. Which brings me to a story in the Bible that talks about this ruler of the synagogue, his name was Jairus. He saw Jesus and fell to his feet and begged Him earnestly saying, his daughter lies at the point of death and He asked Jesus to come and lay hands on her that so she may be healed. Now Jairus was a ruler of the synagogue, but even being a ruler, this is an unfamiliar place. His daughter who he loved was sick unto death. This place that Jairus was in was unknown and not recognized. He fell to the feet of the one who was not a stranger of seeing sick people and healing them. Jairus had enough faith to believe that Jesus can lay his hands on his daughter, and she will be healed. This place was unfamiliar to Jairus, but Jesus was fully acquainted with this situation. The bible say that Jesus went with Jairus. Jairus had to journey to get to the daughter, so the Lord allowed his faith to grow. Jesus did not get to his daughter right away.

On the way there was a woman with an issue of blood that needed Jesus' help. She suffered 12 long years and she realized that Jesus was near, and she went to seek healing. She said if I can just touch the hem of His garment I will be made well and that she did. She was also in an unfamiliar place where she had to do something out of the norm. She touched Jesus' garment. Her faith grew in the unfamiliar place. Because of her faith she received her healing. In the meanwhile, Jairus had to wait and trust that although this may be a delay it is not a denial. While Jesus was speaking with the woman who had the issue, some came from the ruler of the synagogue house who said your daughter is dead. Why trouble the teacher any further. I will like for you all to know that Jairus just experienced a miracle on the way to his daughter. He got a chance to see an impossible made possible. The Lord was allowing Jairus faith to grow. Even when it looks like nothing can happen, it's not too late. We have to trust the Almighty God for He is faithful. Matthew 19:26 NKJV, But Jesus looked at them and said to them, "With men this is impossible, but with God all things are possible". This place was unfamiliar, but Jarius had Jesus with him.

In Mark 5:36, it says, As soon as Jesus heard the word that was spoken, He said to the ruler of the synagogue, "Do not be afraid; only believe". When you are in an unfamiliar place you have to remember what is written. In Hebrews 11:6, But without faith it is impossible to please Him, for he who comes to God must believe that He is a rewarder of them who diligently seek Him. See in the beginning Jairus fell down at Jesus feet. He believed that Jesus could lay hands on his daughter, and she will be healed. In the midst of Jairus trusting, another report came, and he had to grow in faith. Faith in wikibooks.org, faith is the assurance that the things revealed and promised in the word are true, even though unseen, and gives the believer a conviction that what he expects in faith, will come to pass. Jairus had faith! His faith grew in the unfamiliar place. He went from needing healing for his daughter to actually needing her to be raised from the dead. Jesus is faithful to His word. From the onset Jesus went with Jairus. There may have been some things along the way, but it was to Jairus benefit! He got a chance to see a miracle and he got a chance to experience his own supernatural miracle.

I know sometimes people of God, life's journey can present somethings that are unfamiliar and very uncomfortable, but the Lord is using it as an opportunity for us to grow in faith. Through this sermon I want you to look at what Jesus did for Jairus, what He did with the woman with the issue and don't forget what he has already done for you and just know that your faith is growing in the unfamiliar place.

CHAPTER 3

Yesterday move of God was extraordinary, but God is progressive

When we begin to examine our lives through the telescope of the Holy Spirit, we will be able to see how amazing God really is. God has done some great and mighty things that are sometimes indescribable. What God has done in the past cannot compare to what He will do in the future. This chapter is to compel you to believe and know that you have experienced some great and astounding things, but the bible declares in I Corinthians 2:9 KJV, But as it is written,

Eye hath not seen, nor ear heard, neither have entered into the heart of man, the things which God hath prepared for them that love Him. God has something prepared for those that love Him, but we must stay on a journey to experience it. I'm reminded of the book of Joshua, and the children of Israel, they experienced some great, extraordinary and astonishing things. They were free out of Egypt and was able to see a miracle of the Red Sea separating made into walls of water and they were able to cross over on dry land. They were led into the wilderness where God truly took care of them. He fed them manna from heaven and gave them water out of a rock. Their shoes never wore out. God was a cloud by day and fire by night to lead them and guide them. It was an extraordinary move from God.

Extraordinary in a Merriam Webster dictionary means going beyond what is usually regular, or customary. It was not usual the way the Lord was taking care of them. Even in what He was doing that was so extraordinary, God is progressive, He is continuous. He is always waiting for an opportunity to amaze us. In the book of Joshua, we see that God is continuing to do amazing things. God informed Joshua to be strong and courageous. He has some great things in store, but Joshua and the Israelites had to pursue. Many in the wilderness wasn't able to experience all that God had in store for them because of their unbelief.

Those that chose to believe went on to see great and mighty things that they knew not of. In one particular place in Joshua the 6th chapter it talks about the walls of Jericho. The Lord had helped them to cross the Jordan and now they were faced with the wall that was impossible to come down by man. See, when we are faced with life challenges, and we come to a place with this thing that seems as if it is taller than me and God, we have to remember that God never fails. Nothing is greater than God. This wall that they faced was 11 ft. tall and 14 ft. wide, and it look like it was impossible to break, impossible to come down. The Lord is always ahead of what you see. He is Alpha and Omega, the beginning in the end. We must have an ear to hear the instructions that He gives even when it does not make sense. Joshua followed the instructions from the Lord. The Lord told him to march around the wall that stood tall and wide and looked like it will not move. The bible says the instruction was to march in silence. They had to be silent so that unbelief will not come out of their mouths. God's strategy included waiting, walking and no talking. Joshua had to trust God. He had to believe that God's plan will work. Joshua had to remain obedient, although every day he saw the same thing. He was instructed not to talk while they were marching around. God had a plan in place that was supernatural. After following the instructions, it happened. Joshua 6:20, say So the people shouted when the priest blew the trumpets. And it happened with the people heard the sound of the trumpet, and the people shouted with a great shout, that the wall fell down flat. Then the people went up into the city, every man straight before him, and they took the city.

People of God we must keep waiting, keep walking, and keep silent until the Lord release. God knew that the wall was going to come down. It was an extraordinary move from God that the walls came down, but God is progressive. After the walls came down the bible says they took the city. The Lord is progressive! He was doing multiple things at one time for Joshua and the people. God keeps His promise. He will never tell us to do something and not see us through it. Joshua had to remain in obedience no matter what he was looking at. Let's look at this in a way that will help us when we are faced with challenges and circumstances that want to look impossible to overcome. Let us realize that there is nothing impossible for God. He is progressive! He wants to do something that is mine blowing for us, but we must continue to believe and not lose sight of Him. The wall came down and so will every situation that looks impossible for you. Trust in God, wait on Him, and know the move of God was extraordinary, but God is progressive.

.

CHAPTER 4

Reject Satan lies and Act on the Truth!

We see in the book of John 8-chapter verse 31 to 32 AMPLIFIED VERSION it says, So Jesus was saying to the Jews who had believed Him, "If you abide in My word (continually obeying My teachings and living in accordance with them, then) you are truly my disciples. Verse 32 says, And you will know the truth (regarding salvation), and the truth will set you free (from the penalty of sin)". As we look at these two verses, we can see that Jesus is speaking and He's letting those that He's talking know where they stood concerning the knowledge of the truth. Jesus expressed that (if) which means, whether or not you must decide. If you abide in my word. The amplified version explains it to us so we can understand. If we abide meaning (continually obeying Jesus teaching and living in accordance with them, this shows how we are in Christ, true disciples. When we recognize and realize the truth then we can experience true freedom. Let's evaluate our first point that we would like to point out. Point 1. True disciples of Jesus believe. We must believe that He speaks the truth and God and the scriptures is reliable and trustworthy. According to John 14:6 it says, Jesus is the way, the truth and the life no man comes to the Father except through me. Jesus was who He claimed to be. Verse 32 begins with Then you will know the truth. "You refers to those who are true disciples". A true disciple is not just involved but is committed to take up his cross and follow Jesus to the very end. This is a complete and lasting commitment. These true disciples know the truth. More, than that, their eyes are opened to a greater understanding of the truth. In I John 5:20 amplified version says,

And we [have seen and] know [by personal experience], that the Son of God has [actually] come [to this world], and has given us understanding and insight so that we may [progressively and personally] know Him who is true; and we are in him who is true – in His Son Jesus Christ. This is the true God and eternal life. The Apostle John was not speaking from what someone told him, but he was speaking of personal encounter. He seen Jesus, he walked with Jesus, he had a relationship with Jesus, and he truly believed that Jesus was and is the truth. The truth that Jesus disciples receive brings with it freedom. Jesus explain, when you know the truth, it will make you free. The freedom that Jesus offers is a spiritual freedom from the bondage of sin. You are a slave to sin if you do not submit to the truth. The biblical concept of submission is to place oneself under the authority of another. Truth has authority because Jesus is the truth. We as true disciples have to submit to the truth (Jesus Christ) so we can experience the freedom of Jesus explained in verse 32. We must understand that there is an enemy (devil) who does not want you to know the truth. He wants to deceive and lie so we can be bound. He wants us to be restricted and limited. But Jesus wants us to be free indeed. The enemy will lie and try to convince you of that lie because he is a liar. Jesus is the truth. We have to continue to deposit the truth by reading, studying and praying. Staying in close proximity of the truth as possible.

1 Peter 2:16 say Live as free people, but do not use your freedom as a cover or pretext for evil, but (use

it) and live as bondservants of God. There is a place that God desires His people to live. He wants this to be a lifestyle not just a visit sometimes. He wants us to live free. Live means in KJV dictionary, to abide, to dwell; to have settled residents in any place (2) to continue to be permanent; not to perish (3) to be an animated; to have the vital principle. Peter was able to make this statement because this was a place that was permanent for him. There was no other way to live but to live for Christ. It was a permanent decision, he lived free. He didn't use his freedom for time to sin but he uses his freedom so people can see that abiding with Christ you will experience the truth. Peter was a bondservant. A bondservant is a person bound in service without wages. Peter knew the truth and was bound to it. He lived by it, and he communicated it. Jesus is the truth. He wanted those that believed and received Him to follow the truth. Don't deviate from it. The bible reminds us the Holy Spirit will lead us to all truth. We must be determined just as the others in the bible, they knew the truth and from them knowing the truth the truth made them free. Remember whom the Son sets free is free indeed. Walk in this truth. Amen.

CHAPTER 5

Master of Breakthroughs

This particular chapter will be dealing with 2 Samuel 5:17-20. In this chapter we see the David was about to enter into a battle with the Philistines. These people had heard that David was anointed to be king, and they begin to look for David to destroy him. I would like to inform those that may be reading this book, when you give your life to the Lord and surrender to Him with a "Yes", the devil and his demons are disturbed. The reason for them being disturbed is that they know that God's kingdom will be advanced and his kingdom of darkness will be weakened. The enemy looks for ways to destroy us, but we must keep in mind according to Isaiah 54:17 amplified version it says, "No weapons that is formed against you will succeed; And every tongue that rises against you in judgment you will condemn. This (peace, righteousness, security and triumph over opposition) is the heritage of the servants of the Lord, And this is their vindication from Me", says the Lord. Even though this enemy was coming up against David and the enemy is coming up against you, no weapons formed against you shall prosper. It will form, but it will not prosper. David had to go to God. He had to inquire of the Lord saying should I go up against the Philistines. I would like to interject right here! David did something that must be noticed and understood. He inquired of the Lord. That word inquire means in the Oxford dictionary, ask for information from someone. Well David asked God for some information concerning this battle he was about to enter. He wanted to know should he go up against the Philistines. One thing I want to encourage you through this chapter is that David did something, at times we fail to do, "Inquire".

When something catches us by surprise a lot of times we react according to our feelings and emotions. David knew that he had to consult God. He talked to the to the Author and Finisher of his faith. He went to the Source and Sustainer that knows everything. As the Lord released this sermon to me, I begin to look at different things I think about when I said yes to the Lord, and he began to anoint me to do a work for Him. All hell begin to break loose because the enemy do not like anyone that is sincere about the things of God and doing God's will. Just like David, there were many battles I had to go to God. I had to inquire of the Lord on what to do. He was the one with the answer. He was the source of all things. The Lord told David after he inquired, "Go up for I will certainly hand them over to you". Wow this is so amazing to know that the Lord will tell you what to do because he has a plan. This plan is victorious. He wanted to show David that He was the Master of Breakthrough. When we think about the word Master in the Oxford dictionary means Lord; a ruler; one who has supreme dominion. The Lord had to show David that He was supreme ruler, and nothing can overtake God. He is the Master. In 2 Samuel 5:20

amplified it says, So David came to Baal-Perazim, and David defeated them there, and he said, "The Lord has broken through my enemies before me, like a breakthrough of water". So, he named it Baal-perazim (master of breakthroughs). David understood that God was the Master of Breakthrough. He knew that God broke through his enemies. The enemy plans were to destroy David. They wanted to take him out, but God had a plan. As I was looking at this and analyzing these scriptures, I begin to look at Jesus. Jesus came to earth so we can rule again, but Jesus had to endure his enemies that was coming up against Him. I'm reminded of after He was baptized and came out of the water the heavens were opened up and John saw the Spirit of God descending like a dove and alighting upon Him (Jesus) and behold, a voice from heaven said, this is my beloved Son and whom I am well pleased and delighted. This was the anointing that was upon Jesus. Right after this happened the bible says that Jesus was led by the Holy Spirit into the wilderness to be tempted by the devil. Jesus himself had to enter into a battle that the Holy Spirit led Him into. He came out victorious because He did what Holy Spirit lead him to do. Just like David he inquired of the Lord and the Lord released instructions so he can be victorious. Now those that is reading this have accepted salvation and now the Holy Spirit (Master of Breakthrough) is inside of you. There's nothing you can face or be presented with (that may look extremely difficult) our precious and faithful God won't bring us out of. God is the Master. He sent his Son Jesus to die for us and He did not leave us comfortless. He sent the Holy Spirit to live in us, so we will be able to breakthrough anything that may rise up against us. David was anointed to be king. Jesus is the Anointed One and we have been anointed by Jesus through and by Holy Spirit. Just as we see how the enemy tried to prevail, he did not succeed. We have to be like Jesus when He was tempted of satan, He told the enemy what was written, and the enemy had to flee. God is the Master of Breakthroughs and this Master is in you in Jesus name Amen.

CHAPTER 6

Transforming Encounter

We look at this chapter and we will see how we can transform by having an encounter with Jesus. In the book of Romans chapter 12 and verses 1 and 2 in the amplified version, it says, Therefore I urge you, brothers and sisters, by the mercies of God, to present your bodies [dedicating all of yourselves, set apart] as a living sacrifice, holy and well-pleasing to God, which is your rational (logical, intelligent) act of worship. Verse 2 And do not be conformed to this world [any longer with a superficial values and customs], but be transformed and progressively changed [as you mature spiritually] by the renewing of your mind [focusing on godly values and ethical attitude], so that you may prove [for yourselves] what the will of God is, that which is good and acceptable and perfect [in His plan and purpose for you]. This word transform means to change radically in inner character condition, or nature. The Apostle Paul in Romans 12:2 was encouraging believers, do not be conformed to this world, but be transformed by the renewing of your mind. Believers of Jesus Christ should not be conformed to this world. The word conformed in the Oxford dictionary means comply with rules standards or laws. This world system has rules and standards that goes against the word of God. We as followers of Christ have to have a personal encounter with Jesus so we can be transformed. This world is fallen and the only way we are going to withstand we must be transformed.

We need this encounter with Jesus. The word encounter means an unexpected a casual meeting with someone or something. When we have this encounter, it is not planned, but it is something that is wanted. Until we have the unexpected meeting, we will not transform. The Bible tells us that we have to present ourselves a living sacrifice to God. When we offer ourselves to live for the Lord, we begin a process of inner transformation that will lead to an entirely new outlook on life. We present ourselves and then our mind is renewed also. We do this through prayer, studying God's word, by the Power of the Holy Ghost and be progressively transformed into Jesus Christ likeness. As I look at this word I begin to think about the author whose name is Paul. He is able to write Romans 12:1-2 because of his own life experience. In the book of Acts the ninth chapter,

Paul himself had a transformation encounter. He had an unexpected meeting that was not planned. He was on the road to Damascus to persecute the church. When suddenly a light shined down from heaven blinded him of the direction he was going in and knocked him down off his horse. Not only was this done to Paul naturally but there was a spiritual transformation taking place. After Paul's encounter with Jesus, the Lord transformed his life. Paul was never the same. He began to become a follower of Jesus Christ. The Lord turned his whole life around and he was never the same. So, Paul was not just writing about someone else experience, but he was writing about himself. As I write, I myself have had many encounters with Jesus in my life, and I changed drastically. When I decided to surrender (present my body a living sacrifice), I was never the same.

God has changed my whole life. I think about 1 Peter 1:14-16 in the amplified version it says, "[Live] as obedient children [of God]; do not be conformed to the evil desires which governed you in your ignorance [before you know the requirements and transforming power of the good news regarding salvation]. See Peter is letting us know live as obedient children. See you can't obey without the encounter. Before my encounter I did not obey God. I went in my own way to do my own thing just like Paul was on the road to Damascus. People of God there are evil desires which governs you when you are ignorant. This book is to shed light so we will no longer be ignorant. The encounter with Jesus transforms you back into Christ likeness. You will no longer be governed by ignorance. The Gospel (the good news) of Jesus Christ will turn your whole life around. Once you receive salvation through this encounter your life will never be the same. This change that I am presenting to you is for anyone that is willing and want this encounter. Jesus died, was buried, and was resurrected so we can experience this encounter and be transformed. This encounter will change everything about your old you. Let's decide as we read this chapter that you too can experience Jesus in such a great way that you can tell someone and just maybe as he changed me and you we can change someone else. Enjoy the transformation encounter.

CHAPTER 7

Don't let the enemy Hijack your Journey

In this particular chapter, I will like to start off with the bible verse the Lord has opened up to me, Exodus 14:13 NJKV, And Moses said to the People, "do not be afraid, Stand still, and see the salvation of the Lord, which He will accomplish for you today. For the Egyptians whom you see today, you shall see again no more forever. As I looked at and studied this verse the Lord began to highlight some things. Just to give some history on the scene of what is happening. The Lord called and chose Moses to go to Egypt and free His people. Although God knew that this task would be difficult, He empowered Moses to do what He asked him to do. Moses, in fact, did what the Lord said in spite the challenges he faced. He still moved forward in what God told him to do. Moses took a stand and went to the King whose name was Pharaoh and told him to let God's people go.

King Pharaoh had a hard heart. He was very stubborn and rebellious towards God and he did not want to adhere to Moses. So, the Lord sent many plagues, 10 plagues to be exact, and he did not want to listen to Moses. After a while, the last plague was a death angel that came through Egypt and killed all the first-born sons of the people in Egypt. Finally, Pharaoh began to take what Moses was saying and demonstrating serious. After Pharaoh released the children of Israel, He was very angry and changed His mind, so he began to chase after them.

I'm going to pause, because I want to interject something right here. We must understand that Pharaoh was a type of Satan. The devil had us before we gave our life to the Lord. Now that we did, he realized that he doesn't have us no more so he tries to fight to get us back. The devil is a liar! When you get free, you begin to run for your life. According to Romans 6:7 NJKV, For he who has died has been freed from sin. Sin is an enemy and when we left Satan the Lord freed us from the power of sin. He freed us from Satan's grip he had on our life. Now we can be who God has called us to be from the beginning. My whole point is, we liken what the Israelites went through to what we experience today. The devil will try to chase you down to get you back in bondage, but we must keep running and looking forward. In Exodus 14:11-12, it explains how the Israelites got freed then began to murmur and complain. They were explaining to Moses their fears. They couldn't see the plan of God and so they began to blame Moses for what was happening, when in fact, God did have a plan.

Everything that was happening was on purpose for purpose. The bible says in Jeremiah 29:11 NLT, For I know the plans I have for you," says the Lord. "They are plans for good and not for disaster, to give you a future and a hope. Glory Hallelujah!! The Lord had a plan for them and they couldn't see it because they had their eyes fixed on the enemy chasing them (Pharoah and his army). Moses began to speak to them in verse 13 with instructions. First thing Moses said was "Do not be Afraid". The Israelites was afraid of Pharaoh.

They were intimidated by the army that was with Pharaoh but Moses had to stand and trust God as a leader of God's people. He stood on God's promises.

Moses told them this because He knew God had a plan. He didn't know the plan but he knew God had one.

He told them to stand still and see the salvation of the Lord. The Israelites had to get in position in their faith. They had to trust that the rescuer was here and the God of Jacob is right there. People of God, that is just like us. We may be faced with some challenging things but our rescuer is here. I'm reminded right now about when Jesus and the disciples were on the boat and a storm arose. Jesus was sleep and the disciples were panicking. They assumed Jesus didn't care that they were going to perish because of the storm. Jesus told them before they got on the boat that they will go to the other side. The plan was already in place. The storm was not going to kill them, it was to increase their faith. We too get like the Israelites and the disciples. We can't see the plan of God but we have to revert back to what is written, no matter the challenge. Moses told the people this enemy you see today (the Egyptians) you will not see tomorrow. The whole time the enemy was trying to hijack their journey.

He knew they were free and so he tried to get them back in bondage. The word hijack in the oxford dictionary means unlawfully seize an aircraft, ship or vehicle in transit and force it to go to a different destination or use it for one's own purpose. It also means steal (goods) by seizing them in transit; take over something and use it for a different purpose. As I looked at this definition, it made the subject of this chapter and the bible verse in Exodus 14:13 clearer. The Israelites were in transit. They were on their way and Pharaoh tried to hijack their journey. He did not capture them physically but he had them mentally. Pharaoh began to rule them from afar. Just like with us, Satan comes to kill, steal and destroy. He wants us to be paralyzed so we won't make movement. The devil is a liar.

Moses encouraged them to go forward and God will fight for them. I encourage those that are reading this book to go forward and to not look back. Don't let the enemy hijack your journey. Don't let him try to rob you of your peace, your joy and your endurance. You will have an experience just like the Israelites where God will step in and fight for you and all he wants us to do is to not be afraid, stand still and see the salvation of the Lord. We have to learn from the Israelites. They were free from a place but didn't prepare their minds for action. Their minds were still in Egypt. The enemy tries to hijack your journey through fear. We have to get to the place where we realize our only hope is in Jesus. Then we are likely to trust Him. Let's use this chapter as a reminder and a weapon to give Satan what God says about the challenge. He did it for the Israelites.

God parted the red sea for them and drowned their enemies. He will do the same for us. He will free and deliver us and every plan and scheme of the enemy will be drowned. Be encouraged and don't allow the enemy to hijack your Journey.

CHAPTER 8

Run Tell That!!!

When you have a title called "Run tell that" you begin to think, Tell what? In this chapter of the book the Lord is going to explain to us what we should run and tell. In Matthew chapter 28 verses 1-10 we see by this time Jesus was dead for three days. As he promised in the previous chapters, He will rise in 3 days. Mary Magdalene (who was one of Jesus Disciples) and the other Mary came to the tomb where Jesus was laid. When they got there, they saw that the tomb was empty. Jesus was not there. He was risen like He said. As I read this portion of the bible, I begin to imagine in my mind two things happening at one time. First thing is, Mary Magdalene really loved Jesus. Mary Magdalene was not one that said she loved Jesus without action, but she really loved Him.

The Second thing was Her devotion to the relationship she had with Jesus. In the oxford dictionary the word devotion means loving or loyal. The word devotion means giving or showing firm and constant support or allegiance to a person or institution. Wow! This definition really described Mary Magdalene. She showed her love and devotion by walking with Him from the time she met Him, she got delivered from seven demons, she supported Him financially for His ministry, being at the cross when He was being crucified, and to this very moment, coming back to the tomb where He was laid. You have to be in relationship with Jesus to run and tell the good news. Mary got to the tomb to find out He is not there. The 7th verse of Matthew 28th Chapter (New living Translation) says: And now, go quickly and tell his disciples that he has risen from the dead, and he is going ahead of you to Galilee. You will see him there. Remember what I told you. This is where the title is derived from. Run Tell That.

Mary Magdalene's relationship to Jesus caused her to be the first witness to see Jesus risen from the dead. Let's look into how it all began. Jesus' body lies in the tomb for three days, then on the first day of the week an angel comes and rolled away the stone that blocks the door. The purpose was not to release the resurrected Lord, but to permit the disciples to see the place where the body lay!

The angel spoke to the woman (Mary Magdalene) "Don't be afraid!" He said the 7th verse, "Go quickly and tell His disciples that He is risen from the dead".

Jesus was resurrected as He said He would. The woman ran quickly from the tomb.

They were very frightened, but also filled with joy. They rushed to give the disciples the angel's message. As I evaluated this, I look at the words "run tell that" and it is defined as: to exhort someone to go quickly and give information or news to another person. This information that needed to be spread was the Good News of Jesus Christ. We are to be like Mary Magdalene. She took her relationship serious. She could not wait to let the others know that Jesus was risen from the dead. This woman let the people know the Good News of Jesus Christ. The news is the message of Jesus, the Christ, the Messiah, God's ruler promised by the scriptures and specifically, the coming Kingdom of God. This Kingdom of God message is a way of life that is pleasing to God right here on earth.

The good news message is about Jesus' death on the cross and resurrection to restore people's relationship with God. The good news is the descent of the Holy Spirit on believers as the Helper, the resulting promise and hope of being saved for anyone who believes and follow Jesus, and through this, a healing of brokenness of the entire created universe. The time is nearer than it was before, when we first got saved, for Christ to return so we have to run and tell the goodness of Jesus Christ. I think about the word run (which means move at a speed faster than a walk). When you run and tell the goodness you are showing a sense of urgency. It's vital that we spread the good news; that we run and tell it. Many people are lost in the world. Living without the Hope of Glory, living without the risen savior, living aimlessly without the bread of life, the living water. People are perishing right now for a lack of knowledge.

When you do not possess the good news, you can not have life and its abundance. In John 14:6 it says Jesus is the way, the truth and the life. No man come unto the father except by Me. Jesus is the only way to eternal life. There is a mandate for us to Run tell that. We have to let people know who Jesus is and what He came to do for us and that He's coming back again. We must tell those that are lost that they can be found. Tell those that are sick, they can be healed and tell those who are oppressed that Jesus is now risen so they too can rise. Tell the broken hearted that Jesus is ready to mend every broken part of you.

We have to tell the context of the Gospel (Good news) is the imperfection of man in contrast to the perfection of God. The Bible says that Mary Magdalene moved quickly! That word quickly means at a fast speed, rapidly with little or no delay; promptly. She didn't procrastinate but she moved with rhythm of the message. She got the message, and she moved her feet. Once you are clear of the message, you must move your feet. The Gospel saved Mary Magdalene. It was her truth, and she did not stop until she spread the Gospel. It's many things we can Run and tell but let's tell the gospel so lives can be changed, healed and delivered. Amen.

CHAPTER 9

What you know about the truth is being tested

Subtitle: What you know about the truth is on trial

Let's begin with defining the word truth. Truth is in fact a verified indisputable fact. KJV dictionary AV611 says Truth: Conformity to fact or reality; exact accordance with that which is or has been or shall be. The truth of history constitutes its whole value. As born-again believers we believe that every answer to life and the truth on any topic is laid out in the Bible. When you look in the Bible and you read the gospel of John the 8th chapter, verses 31-32 and 36 it says in NKJV, Then Jesus said to those Jews who believed him, "If you abide in my word, you are my disciples indeed. "And you shall know the truth and the truth shall make you free." Verse 36 say, "Therefore if the Son makes you free, you shall be free indeed." In order for us to understand Truth we first have to abide in Jesus' word. This word abide means to remain stable or fixed in a state. It means to continue in a place. Jesus was letting his disciples know that you have to remain stable or fixed in my Word. This will determine your discipleship. When you become a disciple of Jesus Christ, Jesus will open up the truth to you.

According to John 14: 6 NKJV Jesus said to him, "I am the way, the truth, and the life. No one comes to the father except through me. We must understand that Jesus himself is the truth. This is an indisputable fact. This is my reality and for those that have accepted Jesus as their Lord and Savior. The only true freedom is in Jesus Christ. The Bible says in John 15: 5 "I am the vine, you are the branches, He who abides in me, and I in him, bears much fruit; for without Me you can do nothing. This must be your reality because it is the truth. Jesus is our source; he is the vine and we that have been born again are the branches. We must continue throughout time to remain in Jesus because apart from the vine (Jesus) we can't do nothing. So, as we think about the subject of this chapter and the subtitle, we see that the test right now is the truth. Many things are happening in the world and because of these things, many question the truth. The Lord showed me through His word that what we know about the truth is being tested. If we are Christ disciples indeed, then we should know the truth. This word "know" in definition means to perceive with certainty; to understand clearly, to have a clear and certain perception of truth, fact, or anything that actually exist according to KJV dictionary AV611. So, this lets me know that I must be clear and certain of the truth. You must know that Jesus is the truth and know that according to what is spoken in the written logos (Word of God) that it is certain it is trustworthy and reliable.

Being born again assures you of this truth but you must also believe. Trials and tribulations are to make you more aware of the truth. It helps you to depend upon it when it seems like the truth is not working in a particular situation. You have to know in those trying times that the truth will stand. Jesus is the truth, and the truth is the word of God and Jesus is the word. When this becomes your reality and surrounds your atmosphere nothing can stand up against it. The enemy is here to kill, steal, and destroy but Jesus came that we might have a life and have it more abundantly. This is our truth no matter how the enemy strategize to steal our truth and replace it with false information. We have to hold fast to what we know about the truth. As disciples of Jesus Christ, Jesus himself declare to those that know him, that we shall know the truth and the truth will make us free. See, we have to grab hold to this truth and be free. Jesus promised according to his word, therefore whom the Son makes free you shall be free indeed. Our true freedom is in Christ, and this is the truth. And Galatians 5:1 NIV it says, it is for freedom that Christ has set us free. Stand firm, then and do not let yourselves be burdened again by a yoke of slavery. When Jesus free you from not knowing the truth to knowing the truth, do not go back into that place of slavery before you knew the truth.

See, it is the truth that makes you free. The word of God is the truth and because of Jesus Christ we have victory through the truth because the truth has made us free. Amen!

CHAPTER 10

The word of God is not for the Occasional but for those that are Permanent.

Jesus, in His earthly ministry, gave an extended amount of parables. The word parable means from the English language Learners dictionary, a short story that teaches a moral or spiritual lesson. These stories are told by Jesus Christ and are recorded in the Bible. In Matthew 13th chapter verses 10- 13, it talks about the purpose of parables. The 10th verse says, And the disciple came and said to him, why do you speak to them in parables? The 11th verse, He answered and said to them, because it has been given to you to know the mysteries of the kingdom of heaven, but to them it has not been given. 12th verse say, for whoever has, to him more will be given, and he will have abundance but who ever does not have even what he has will be taken away from him. 13th verse say therefore I speak to them in parables, because seeing they do not see, and Hearing they do not hear, nor do they understand.

When Jesus spoke parables, He wanted to reveal himself through a story. Only those that have accepted Him, will He reveal to them what the story is really about. So those that was not interested, it just remained a story. Although the story had a moral and spiritual lesson, there was some that didn't want a relationship with Jesus. It was a crowd and many was following Jesus for all sorts of reasons.

So, Jesus will tell stories and if they were interested and became disciples, He would reveal the truth of what the story was about but to those that didn't want a relationship it remained to be a story. The Kingdom of heaven is a place that only those that are born again can dwell. Those that are of this place can know the mysteries of that kingdom. Jesus came to release the kingdom to those that accept Him. Unfortunately, many didn't receive Jesus. He always made himself available.

In the beginning of this chapter, Jesus was giving a story about a Sower that went out to sow. As the Sower went out to sow some of the seeds fell by the wayside and birds came in devoured them. Some fell on stony places where they did not have much earth and they immediately sprang up because they had no depth of earth. But when the sun was up there scorched and because they had no root, they withered away.

Some fell among thorns in the thorns sprang up and choked them, but others fell on good ground, yielded a crop, some a hundred-fold some sixty and some thirty. Jesus gave this moral story, and it was full of purpose to those that had an ear to hear. Jesus was the sower and seed was the word of God. He was trying to let them know their present condition. He was explaining how He was sowing seed and how he was giving everyone an opportunity to receive His word. He came for all humans, no matter what your condition was, your race, etc. He came to sow the word in the lives of the people so they can change. Jesus is not wasteful, so He gave stories so that if you became interested, He could open the story up for you and explain it like He did to His disciples. He told his disciples it has been given to you to know the mysteries of the kingdom of heaven but to them it has not been given.

The them that Jesus was talking about was those that was not really interested in what Jesus was talking about. Jesus begins to explain the parable to the disciples. He let them know when anyone hears the word of the kingdom and does not understand it, then the wicked one comes and snatches away what was sown in his heart. This is he who received seed by the wayside. When the word is given, we have to strive to protect that word because the adversary does not want us to understand God's word. That's why he tries to make us so busy that we won't attend Bible study or Sunday school because the enemy does not want us to get an understanding. The Bible declares in Hosea 4:6, My people perish for lack of knowledge. The enemy don't want us to know so he will try to snatch away that word.

Then Jesus begins to explain to them the seed that was on stony places. This is he who hears the word and immediately receives with joy, yet he has no root in himself but endures only for a while for tribulations or persecution arises because of the word immediately he stumbles. Beloved, we must let this word of God take root in us. We can't just be excited when we hear the word, but we must continue that excitement when tribulation and persecution come. The word is a seed and that seed has to go inside of our hearts and permeate the atmosphere of our hearts. When it goes in there, it will begin to change our perspective, our outlook on things. The word will begin to stand taller than any tribulation or persecution. Jesus begins to explain about the seed that fell among the thorns. He said the person that hears the word and the cares of this world, and the deceitfulness of riches chokes the Word and he became unfruitful. The Bible says in Jeremiah 4, break up the fallow ground; and do not sow among thorns. Jeremiah was letting them know to clear the field of weeds before sowing on it. We have to prepare our hearts when the word of God is being sowed. We have to clear all things that we tried to choke God's word. You can't get focus on riches. For the love of money is the root to all evil. You have to allow that word to go in, as said previously, and let it dwell in every area of your life so that when trouble shows up you can use what has been deposited inside you to crush that thing that's trying to overtake you.

Then Jesus said the one that receives seed on good ground is he who hears the word and understands it. Who indeed bears fruit and produces some a hundred-fold, sixty-fold and thirty. Jesus is letting us know that when the word of God gets in you (us) that is good ground. Those that did not just show up but really took the word in and applied that word to his or her life and now the evidence is fruit. It produces love, joy, peace, long-suffering, kindness, goodness, faithfulness, gentleness, and self-control. The Lord allows his word to go forth because He knows that if you were to truly receive it, that word will change your life.

The word of God is precious and is to be valued. Jesus only reveals word to those interested. Only to those that want to produce from it. This word is not for the occasional but for those that are permanent with Jesus. Not every now and then in again but those that are truly followers of Jesus Christ, Jesus separated his disciples from the crowd. There is a separation between those that are interested and those that are not. If you want Jesus, He is available. He showed up to the multitude no matter the reason for coming. He still made himself available. He was willing to turn the story into revelation only to those that were his disciples. We cannot be occasional and want God's revealed truth. We must be permanently on board with Jesus and then we will understand and comprehend what the Lord is revealing to those that believe. Amen.

CHAPTER 11

Hold onto your progress in your process.

There are many things that can come and tempt you to let go of the progress you made in Christ. You must determine in your mind that you are going to hold on tight and not let go of your progress in your process. Let us consider Philippians 3:12 (amplified version) it says, Not that I have already obtained it (this goal of being Christ like) or have already been made perfect, but I actively press on so that I may take hold of that (perfection) for which Christ Jesus took hold of me and made me his own. This verse is apostle Paul speaking inspired by the Holy Spirit. He is opening up a revelation of progress in his process. He is showing us that he is making progress, but he has not yet obtained all the fullness of being Christlike. He was working on it every day. He was pressing on. He knows that it was a process. We too have to understand that when you are in Christ, he is cleansing you as you journey. If you look at the progress, and how it is defined, you see it means forward or onward movement toward a destination. Move forward or onward in space or time. Going forward: to continue doing something.

So now we see that Paul was in movement to his destination. He was not there yet but was on his way. We to must understand that when you are journeying with Christ it takes time to look like Him. You have to grow to look like him. That is all a part of your progress. In your process, when we look at the word process, it implies that there is a manufacturing process in place, where products are created under a standardized and ongoing production system. We must understand that there is a manufacturer, and we are the product. He put an ongoing production system inside of us. When he created us, the Bible says God said let us make man in our image to be like us. He had already had in mind what we were going to be and what we were going to do. Men have fallen since this process and Jesus had to come so we can get back into looking like him. Now Paul is showing us through scripture that he's in movement. He's taking action to be like Jesus. He knew he was not perfect but understood if he actively pressed on that he may hold on that perfection for which Christ Jesus had took hold of him.

Jesus was showing through Paul's life, and lives of others in the Bible, that life is a process. You will make progress while you are journeying, but you must hold onto it. Don't allow anyone to discourage you to make you think you have not progressed. There is progression in God. When we are in Christ we progress. If you look at first Corinthians 9:24 it says, Do you not know that in a race all the runners run (their very best to win) but only one receive the prize? Run (your race) in such a way that you may seize the prize and make it yours!

We have to look at this Bible verse and put it in our hearts. We are all in this race called life. We must continue to run this race and remain faithful to God. Look at the progress you made since You have been running for Jesus. Hold on to how much you progressed. Don't let trials and tribulations determine your victory.

You have to know you have victory already. We are moving forward to look like the original us that he made in the beginning. He has to work some things out of us, but that's okay. Yield to the clean up crew (the Holy Spirit). Let him clean you and make you more and more in his image and likeness. As we continue to evaluate the Scriptures, we cannot help but to look at our brother David in the Bible. David was a man after God's own heart. David made plenty of mistakes during his process. He was determined to hold onto the progress that was already made. The Lord helped David win many wars and battles. He helped David through many difficult challenges, but David had to hold to his progress each time. He had to stay in the process. We too have to fight to stay in the process. We had to persevere to know that God, being the manufacturer, knows the product He made. He himself will see to it that we will finish. David didn't give up. He kept going. David had to rely on the true and living God. He made songs to keep him encouraged and focused. Just think about it, you too have to focus on winning. Don't allow your flesh to make you think you can't finish. You can and you will. David and Paul had to hold on. That means to restrain from escape, to keep fast, to retain, to embrace, to connect. to keep from separation.

Don't let what you have already progressed in escape you!! You must embrace it, retain it, grasp or support. I use myself as an example. I've been born again for 24 years. I went through many challenges and had many battles, but I never gave up. I had to hold on to the progress.

Every time I got through or over something I had to hold on to that for the next time. God is faithful. His grace is truly sufficient. I had days when I felt like I was not going to pull through. I tell you Jesus always showed up. He would let me know keep going. The Lord know that I was his product and I needed to move forward toward a destination. I have not yet arrived to Christlike, just as Paul said, but I'm pressing on. I love Jeremiah 29:11, for I know the thoughts that I think toward you, says the Lord, thoughts of peace and not of evil, to give you a future and a hope. The Lord has a plan for his people, and we have to hold on, grasp really tight, to the progress in our process because he wants to give us a future and a hope.

Let's continue to go forward toward our destination. Paul says Philippians 3:14, I press toward the goal for the prize of the upward call of God in Christ Jesus. There is a goal that is set in front of all of us and we have to keep going to reach it. Stay focused and move forward in Jesus' name, amen.

CHAPTER 12

Refused to stop

All of us must realize on this journey called life, we have to make up in our minds that we will not stop until we are finished. In the book of James 1:12 it reminds us, God blesses those who patiently endure testing and temptation. Afterwards, they will receive the crown of life that God has promised to those who loves him. James was writing to the church to encourage them. He wanted them to recognize that you are blessed if you patiently endure testing in temptation. Test and trials will result in endurance and patience. When we patiently endure trials, the results will be maturity, and a faith that lacks nothing. First, let's consider the word patience. In the Oxford dictionary it means the capacity to accept or to tolerate delay, trouble or suffering without getting angry or upset. As I look for further meaning from a biblical standpoint from the KJV dictionary it means the sufferings of afflictions, Pain, Toil, Calamity, Provocation Or Other evil, with a calm, unruffled temper, endurance without murmuring or fretfulness. When we begin to evaluate the meaning of patience, we can begin to understand the Apostle James.

This is part of the reason why God blesses those who patiently endure testing in temptation. Patience all by itself can only be demonstrated by the help of the Holy Spirit. In the midst of affliction, toil, pain, calamity, tolerating delay, provocation, etc., we must remain calm and have a controlled temper, only the Lord can help us to achieve. When everything is going our way, patience is easy to demonstrate. The true test of patience comes when our rights are violated. Some may feel they have a right to get upset in the face of irritations and trials. Patience will reveal our faith in God's timing. In the book of Galatians 6:9 in NKJV, do not grow weary while doing good for in due season we will reap if we do not lose heart. We must refuse to stop! Continue to do good and not lose heart. Don't allow our trials to dictate how we feel. Allow your test and trials to produce endurance. We know patience does not develop overnight. God's power and goodness are crucial to the development of patients. Colossians 1:11 states being strengthened with all power, according to his glorious might for all endurance and patience with joy. We are all strengthened by him to great endurance and patience.

Also in James 1:3-4 it encourages us to know that trials are God's way of perfecting our patience. Our patience is then, further developed and strengthened by resting totally in God's perfect will and timing. Even in the face of evil men who succeed in their ways, when they carry out the wicked schemes according to Psalm 37:7. In the face of trials and test we must refuse to stop. Even when things don't look like it is moving fast enough, we can't give up. We must deny that thought and continue to tolerate delay. When something is delayed it doesn't mean denial. Continue to hold on to this word in James and let it become your reality. We must endure tests and trials.

When we look at the word endure in the Merriam Webster, it means to undergo especially without giving in. Sometimes our trial and test can be very challenging, but our God will not allow us to be tempted above what we can handle. Testing carries the idea of proving genuineness. Trials serve as a discipline to purge faith debris, string away what is not real or false. We had to tolerate the moment that we are in and not give in to it.

When you think about our Lord and Savior Jesus Christ, the Bible says He was led into the wilderness by the spirit to be tempted by the devil. Jesus refused to stop even though Satan came to tempt him to get him off focus, but he was determined to endure. Jesus uses the word of God as his weapon during the time of being tested. No matter how difficult the challenge was, Jesus persevered, He did not stop. He demonstrated for us that we can make it all the way through. Paul told Timothy to endure hardship as a great soldier. Paul knew that trials and test will come to Timothy, but Timothy had to strive to remember what apostle Paul had taught him. He was to remember what he was taught and what he studied. In Matthew 19:26, Jesus looks at them and said, with men this is impossible, but with God all things are possible. Jesus was teaching his disciples that nothing was impossible for God. His strength is supernatural. You can do it and you can make it. These tests are here to prove that you are genuine in your faith. It is saying you really believe, and you trust God's timing. We must refuse to stop. When the enemy comes to tell you, this is too much for you to handle, you let him know that God's strength is made perfect in weakness.

The word of God is what helps you get through your difficulties. There is a reward for refusing to stop. When you keep going and you endure the Bible say afterward, they will receive a crown of life that God promised of those who love him. Paul told Timothy, I fought a good fight, I kept the faith and finished my course. He refused to stop. When the odds were against him, he held fast to the word that was written on his heart. He remembered the words he preached to others that brought Deliverance. Now he had to use the same words. Paul knew his final destination. He knew The Lord was with him. He did not give into the threats, he did not get out of position and start writing the churches recklessly, but he stayed the course. He didn't give into what he was hearing. He stayed with the word of God. He didn't stop until it was over. Paul received the crown of life for not stopping. There is a reward according to Colossians 3:23-24 it says whatever you do, work at it with all your heart since you know that you will receive an inheritance from the Lord as a reward. It's the Lord Christ you are serving. Stay focused and refused to stop. Don't give up. Don't give into the temptation not to finish. Refused to stop. In Jesus name, amen.

Printed in the United States
by Baker & Taylor Publisher Services